BATS

BIGGEST! LITTLEST!

Sandra Markle

BOYDS MILLS PRESS

AN IMPRINT OF HIGHLIGHTS

Honesdale, Pennsylvania

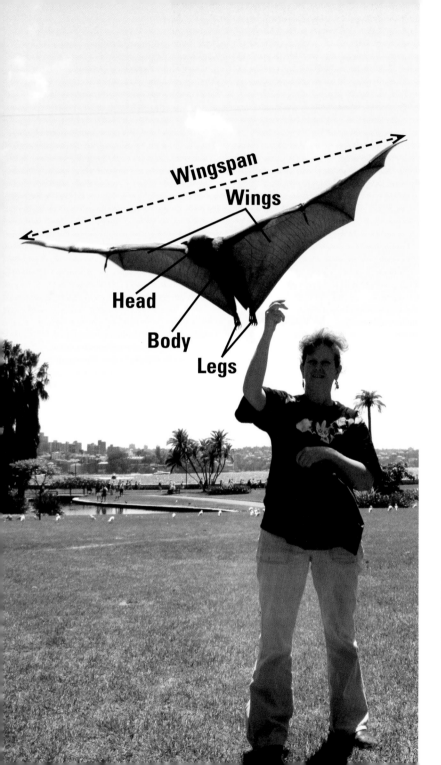

Some bats are big.

This is a Gray-Headed Flying Fox.
It is one of the biggest kinds of bats.
Its wingspan stretches about 3 feet (1 meter).
There are about 60 different kinds of
Flying Foxes. Some have a wingspan slightly
longer than the average bathtub.

*Big or little, all bats have a head, body,
two legs, and two wings.*

Some bats are little.

This is a Bumblebee Bat.
It's the world's littlest kind of bat.
It weighs about as little as an American penny.
Its wingspan is just 6 inches (about 15 centimeters).
That's only an inch longer than a soda-pop can.

So why be big?

For some bats, being big means staying safe.

This Great Fruit-Eating Bat's big size means predators, like owls, usually leave it alone. The Great Fruit-Eating Bat is also strong enough to fly while carrying fruit like this fig.

It eats as it flies.

Or it roosts in a tree and dines safely out of sight.

Great Fruit-Eating Bats are a big help to trees. While they fly, they mash fruit to swallow the juice and spit out the pulp and seeds. Some of the seeds sprout where they land. Then new trees grow up without being crowded around the parent tree.

A Great Fruit-Eating Bat can have a wingspan of 1½ feet (½ meter).

With its wings folded, a Common Vampire Bat is so small it could fit in a teacup.

So why be small?

For some bats, being small means eating food too little for bigger bats to bother with.

For a Common Vampire Bat, though, being small lets it sneak up on big prey like cattle and drink their blood.

Vampire Bats have thicker, stronger hind legs than most bats. So, like this bat, they can jump to reach their prey.

Next, the bat bites and licks the wound. The bat's spit has chemicals that keep the blood flowing as the bat drinks its blood meal.

No matter its size, a bat's wings are the biggest parts of its body.

They're made up of skin stretched over the bones of its front limbs.

A bat can move its finger-like parts the way you move your fingers, one at a time.

So when a bat flies, it can change its wing shape to turn, hover, and flip.

It can also climb up or down a tree trunk.

Thumb

See the bones and blood vessels in this Pallid Bat's wings.

Bats and birds fly very differently. To flap like a bird, keep your fingers together and move your arms up and down. To flap like a bat, spread your fingers and move just your hands up and down.

Wings also help a bat cool off and stay warm.

As a bat flies, the blood flowing through its wings loses heat to the air.

So even though flapping makes a bat heat up, it doesn't get too hot.

While resting, a bat also flaps its wings if it needs to cool off.

To stay warm, a bat wraps its wings around itself to trap its body heat.

Big, leathery wings make a good raincoat for this Gray-Headed Flying Fox.

Some bats have big body parts.

A Spectacled Flying Fox's big eyes let it see very well at night.

Its long nose is packed with sensors that give it a keen sense of smell.

So, as the bat flies through the dark, it easily homes in on fruit to eat.

It also searches out flowers to feed on nectar, the sweet juice that flowers produce.

This bat's big wings let it fly as far as 30 miles (48 kilometers) in a night.

So, when searching for food, it can cover longer distances than many other kinds of bats.

The light-colored circles around this bat's eyes make it look as if it's wearing glasses. That's how the Spectacled Flying Fox got its name.

Big bumps on their lips give Fringe-Lipped Bats their name. The bumps are packed with chemical sensors. These sensors help the bats make sure they bite only what's safe to eat.

Fringe-Lipped Bats have big ears. That makes them good listeners.

This bat catches frogs by homing in on the calls the frogs make to attract a mate. A Fringe-Lipped Bat can even tell poisonous frogs from other frogs by their calls.

This Western Pipistrelle is another bat with big ears.
It hunts flying insects.

It doesn't just listen for bug voices, though.

While the bat flies, it opens its mouth and makes high-pitched clicks. Then it listens for echoes, those sounds that strike something and bounce back.

Sensing the world by listening for echoes is called *echolocation.*

When the Western Pipistrelle senses flying insects, it swoops. Then it snags a bug meal out of the air.

When a bat blasts out a sound, muscles squeeze its middle ear. It's like clamping your hands over your ears. As soon as the bat stops making the sound, the muscles relax. Then the bat is ready to listen for the echo.

The Western Pipistrelle is the smallest bat in
North America. Its wingspan is only about
8 inches (20 centimeters).

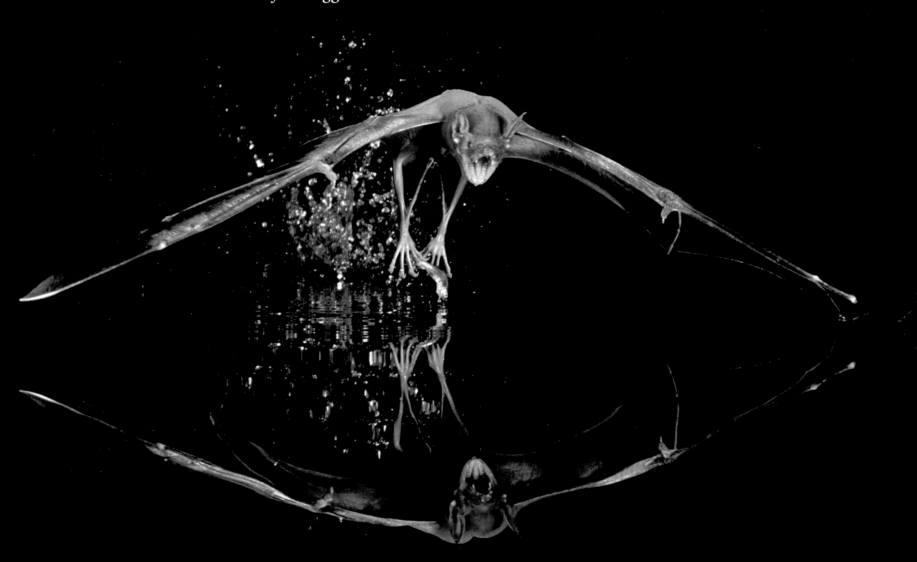

With a wingspan of 3 feet (about 1 meter), the Greater Bulldog Bat is one of the biggest bats in North America.

Many other kinds of bats also use echolocation.

This Greater Bulldog Bat uses echolocation to catch fish.
The bat has its mouth open wide to blast out sounds.
Flying low over water, it listens for echoes bouncing
off ripples.
That's how it senses the fish swimming just below
the surface.
The Greater Bulldog Bat has longer legs and bigger claw-
tipped toes than most bats have.
It can catch prey too slippery for other bats.

The Greater Bulldog Bat has big cheek pouches. When it catches a fish, it stuffs the meal into its cheeks to carry it. The bat may eat while it flies. Or it may fly to a tree and hang upside down while it dines.

The Tube-Lipped Nectar Bat counts on another really big body part to survive. That's its super-long tongue.

Such a long tongue lets it lick nectar from the bottom of extra-long tube-shaped flowers. So the Tube-Lipped Nectar Bat can eat food that's out of reach for other kinds of bats.

Compared to its body size, the Tube-Lipped Nectar Bat has the world's longest tongue. In fact, the bat's tongue is longer than its body.

The tongue is so long that the base is attached inside the rib cage instead of the mouth. When not in use, this long tongue lies next to the bat's heart.

The Tube-Lipped Nectar Bat has a big space between its front teeth. It barely has to open its mouth to flick its long tongue in and out.

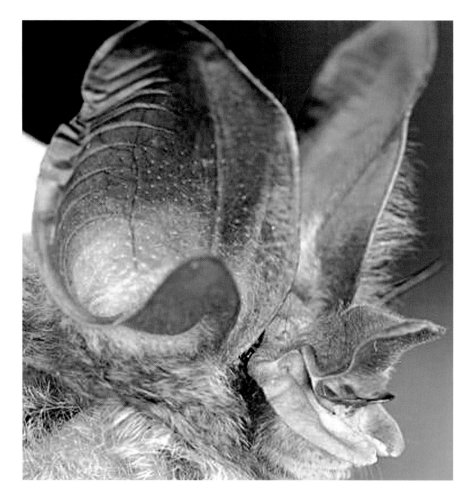

This bat may fly to hunt. Or it may hang from a branch and make noises while twisting one way, then another. When it senses an insect, it swoops to catch its prey. That way it saves energy while it hunts.

Some bats have little body parts that make a big difference.

The Bourret's Horseshoe Bat has flaps of skin around its nose. When searching for flying insects, it snorts out high-pitched noises.

Just as a flashlight shines a beam of light, the flaps around this bat's nose focus its sounds.

Bats without nose flaps hear echoes from all directions at once.

The Bourret's Horseshoe Bat hears echoes from only one direction at a time.

The thumb-sized Spix's Disk-Winged Bat can support its entire weight with just one disk.

At the base of each thumb and ankle, the Spix's Disk-Winged Bat has a little cup-shaped disk. It acts like a suction cup.

The pull is enough to stick the disk to smooth surfaces, like leaves.

Inside a curled leaf, the Spix's Disk-Winged Bat stays dry in the rain. It also hides from predators, like owls and snakes.

Whatever their size, many kinds of bats gather in groups.

Honduran White Bats do more than just hang out together.

They make a tent they can share.

To do that, the bats bite the side veins of a large banana leaf.

When enough veins are snapped, the sides of the leaf flop down.

Then the little bats stay dry when it rains. They're also shielded from the hot sun and hidden from snakes and other predators.

With a wingspan of just 4 inches (about 10 centimeters), Honduran White Bats are the world's smallest fruit-eating bats. Tiny as they are, they have bigger bodies than Bumblebee Bats and weigh more than twice as much.

Female Free-Tailed Bats gather together to have babies in nursery caves.

When the mothers leave to hunt insects, the babies stay home, huddled in big groups.

Then, if a predator like a snake comes into the cave, each baby has a better chance of escaping. There is safety in being part of a big group.

Every baby Mexican Free-Tailed Bat has its own scent and call. That lets each mother find her baby.

Gray-Headed Flying Foxes usually have only one baby a year.

For baby bats, being little means being in the greatest danger of any time in their lives.

That's why a mother Gray-Headed Flying Fox takes advantage of being big and strong to keep her little baby close.

When she flies in search of flowers and fruit, she lets her baby cling to her fur. Then she carries her baby with her.

For a baby bat, growing up is all about becoming as big or as little as the bat needs to be.

Some are little.

Others are BIG.

A bat's size is its very life.

That is how each different kind of bat has adapted to survive in its own special part of the world.

Check this map to see where the bats in this book were photographed. They may also be found in other parts of the world. Bats live on every continent except Antarctica. The measurements provided are the maximum length of each bat's forearm (wrist to elbow length) when the wing is folded. This measurement is one of the key ways scientists compare bats. A bat can move its finger-like parts and change its wing shape and thus its wingspan in lots of little ways. But the forearm length never changes.

Western United States
Pallid Bat
(2.3 inches/6 centimeters)
Townsend's Big-Eared Bat
(1.8 inches/4.7 centimeters)
Western Pipistrelle
(1.2 inches/3.1 centimeters)

Texas
Mexican Free-Tailed Bat
(1.8 inches/4.5 centimeters)

Mexico
Common Vampire Bat
(2.6 inches/6.5 centimeters)
Greater Bulldog Bat
(3.5 inches/8.9 centimeters)

Costa Rica
Honduran White Bat
(1.2 inches/3.1 centimeters)

Panama
Fringe-Lipped Bat
(2.6 inches/6.5 centimeters)
Great Fruit-Eating Bat
(3 inches/7.8 centimeters)
Spix's Disk-Winged Bat
(1.5 inches/3.8 centimeters)

Ecuador
Tube-Lipped Nectar Bat
(1.6 inches/4 centimeters)

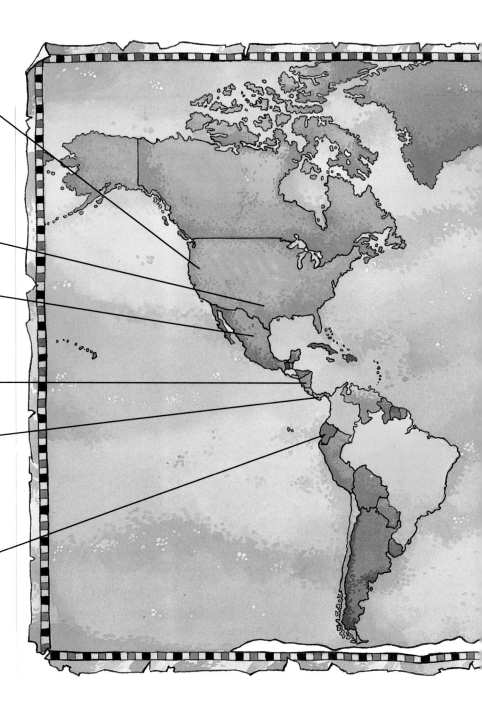

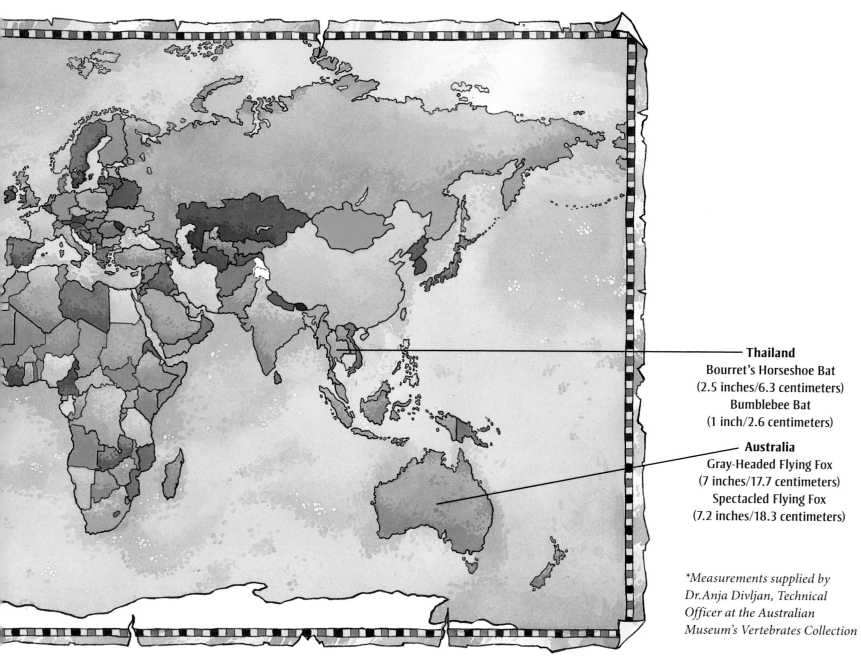

Thailand
Bourret's Horseshoe Bat
(2.5 inches/6.3 centimeters)
Bumblebee Bat
(1 inch/2.6 centimeters)

Australia
Gray-Headed Flying Fox
(7 inches/17.7 centimeters)
Spectacled Flying Fox
(7.2 inches/18.3 centimeters)

*Measurements supplied by
Dr.Anja Divljan, Technical
Officer at the Australian
Museum's Vertebrates Collection*

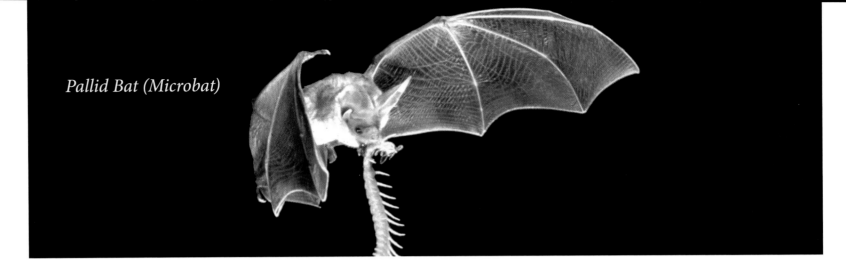

Pallid Bat (Microbat)

Two Bat Groups

Bats are divided into two groups, megabats (big bats) and microbats (little bats). All the megabats are types of Flying Foxes. There are lots of different kinds of microbats, such as Horseshoe Bats, Bulldog Bats, and Vampire Bats. The group names can be confusing. Some microbats are actually bigger than some megabats. The clearest difference between the two groups is what the bats eat and how they find their food. Megabats mainly eat nectar, pollen, or fruit; they mainly depend on sight and smell to find food. Microbats usually catch insects and animal prey; they mainly depend on hearing and echolocation to find food.

No matter what group they belong to, bats play a key role in the world. Bats that drink nectar help move pollen (male reproductive cells) from flower to flower. By carrying pollen, bats help plants produce seeds that will grow into new plants. Bats that eat insects and other animals help control pests. Otherwise, those pests could destroy important food crops or spread diseases.

Bat Words You Learned

Echolocation. The means of sensing the world based on echoes, bounced-back sounds.

Nectar. Sweet liquid produced by flowers.

Nursery. A place for the care of babies.

Predator. An animal that catches other animals, its prey, in order to eat and live.

Prey. An animal that a predator catches and eats.

Wing. A movable body part used mainly for flight.

Wingspan. When the wings are stretched out, the distance between wingtips.

For More Information

To find out more about bats, check out the following books and websites.

Books

Carney, Elizabeth. *Bats*. National Geographic Readers Series. Washington, DC: National Geographic, 2010. Explore a world of amazing facts about bats.

Carson, Mary Kay. *The Bat Scientists*. Scientists in the Field Series. Boston: Houghton Mifflin Books for Children, 2010. Go along with bat researcher Merlin Tuttle as he studies different kinds of bats in a variety of habitats.

Markle, Sandra. *Little Lost Bat*. Watertown, MA: Charlesbridge, 2006. This fictional story shares real-life facts about the lives of Mexican Free-Tailed Bats. Discover how orphaned babies are adopted by stepmother bats.

Markle, Sandra. *Outside and Inside Bats*. Outside and Inside Series. New York: Walker Books, 1997. Learn about bat traits and behavior.

Websites*

Basic Facts About Bats
defenders.org/bats/basic-facts
Listen to bat sounds and explore facts about different kinds of bats.

Bat Activities
kidzone.ws/animals/bats/activities.htm
Pictures of bats to print out and color while learning key facts about bats. Don't miss the online jigsaw puzzles: click and drag to put pictures together.

Bat Conservation International
batcon.org
Visit the Bat Conservation International (BCI) Photo Gallery to view pictures of lots of different kinds of bats. Don't miss the activities at "All About Bats/Kidz Cave."

Bat Kids
bats.org.uk/pages/batsforkids.html
Lots of information about bats and ways you can help your local bats. Includes games and things to make and do.

Bats4Kids
bats4kids.org
Find the answers to frequently asked questions about bats and how you can help your local bats. Also includes games and links to other sites with bat information.

*Active at time of publication

For Nancy Bourne and her students at Beacon Cove Intermediate School, Jupiter, Florida

Cover photograph shows Townsend's Big-Eared Bat. Read pages 13 through 15 to find out how having big ears can help a bat.

Photographs: Cover, 6, 9, 16, 30: J. Scott Altenbach; Cover (inset), 3: Merlin Tuttle/Getty; Back Cover, 1, 10, 27: Vivien Jones; 2: Anja Divljan; 5, 13, 21: Christian Ziegler/Minden; 12: Theo Allofs/Minden; 15: Michael Durham/Minden; 18, 19: Nathan Muchhala; 20: Rolf Mueller; 23: Konrad Wother/Minden; 24: Robert W. Mitchell; 25: Nick Edards.

Acknowledgments: The author would especially like to thank the following experts for sharing their expertise and enthusiasm: Dr. Scott Altenbach, University of New Mexico; Susan Barnard, Basically Bats Wildlife Conservation Society; Dr. Anja Divljan, Australian Museum; and Dr. Rolf Mueller, Virginia Tech. A special thank-you to Skip Jeffery for his help and support throughout the creative process.

Note to Parents and Teachers: The books in the BIGGEST! LITTLEST! series encourage children to explore their world. Young readers are encouraged to wonder. Then kids are guided to discover how animals depend on their special body features to be successful in their particular environment.

Boyds Mills Press, Inc.
815 Church Street
Honesdale, Pennsylvania 18431
Printed in Mexico

ISBN: 978-1-59078-952-0
LCCN: 2012947937
First edition
The text of this book is set in Minion.

10 9 8 7 6 5 4 3 2 1

"All organisms have external parts. Different animals use their body parts in different ways to see, hear, grasp objects, protect themselves, move from place to place, and seek, find, and take in food, water, and air. Plants also have different parts (roots, stems, leaves, flowers, fruits) that help them survive, grow, and produce more plants."
—From the National Research Council report *A Framework for K-12 Science Education*, which is the basis for the Next Generation Science Standards.